everything in life is a ...

Journey To The Top

Motivated Publishing Ventures

Journey To The Top

Book and design cover by RAS
Original photography by John A. Stewart, (unless otherwise noted)
Cover: Early morning sunrise over Ama Dablam
Manufactured in Canada

ISBN 978-0-9781233-4-5

"It is not the mountain we conquer, but ourselves."

— Sir Edmund Hillary

 # Acknowledgements

I would like to first thank my wife Julie. Your love and support have been a source of ongoing strength and support for me. Thank you also for your unwavering encouragement as I continue on my journey in my life.

Thanks also to my two fabulous children Sydney and Scott. You add enjoyment to my life that keeps me energetic and enthused. I wish for both of you, all that you truly desire as you continue on your journey through life.

This is book is dedicated to Julie, Sydney and Scott. I love you.

Thank you for being you.

"You don't have to be a fantastic hero to do certain things – to compete.
You can be just an ordinary chap, sufficiently motivated"

— Sir Edmund Hillary

Contents

Preface

If someone were to ask me to describe myself, the first thing I would say is that I am just an ordinary guy. I was raised in Southern Ontario, Canada, in a typical middle class family. My parents raised me and two older sisters in a loving and caring family. I went to church and each Sunday night we would have a big family dinner in the dining room, instead of the kitchen where we normally ate. The Stewart family gatherings have always been interesting with plenty of fun and laughter. When people meet my father for the first time, they comment that "the apple doesn't fall far from the tree." It is very apparent after meeting my father that he is definitely the source of my sense of humor.

After graduating from McMaster University with a Bachelor of Arts degree, I wasn't sure exactly what I wanted to do, but I figured a career in sales would be a good idea. After graduating, I entered into the family's manufacturing and distribution business, and after six years I left to pursue a career in financial planning.

I am very fortunate to say that my high school sweetheart, Julie, became my wife and after twenty two years of marriage she means as much to me now as she ever did. Something that many young couples take for granted, having a family, didn't come so easily for Julie and I. In 1988, we made the decision to start a family. Little did we know at that time that it would take six years to happen. Julie had difficulties with her pregnancies reaching full term. Throughout those six years, we would have to endure six miscarriages and the still birth of our son Steven. Losing Steven, after having so many losses before him, was an extreme low point for Julie and I. People marveled at how we were able to get through it. Two days after the loss of Steven, with Julie still in the hospital, I was talking to our close friend and neighbor, Sue. She asked me how I was coping and I remember saying, "If God is going to push me over, I'm going to make sure that I fall forward." I realized that when faced with a severe hardship you just do what you have to do to cope. For me, moving forward with a positive attitude was a necessity.

Almost two years to the day after our loss, we were blessed with the birth of our daughter Sydney. Fifteen months after that we were blessed again, this time with our son Scott. Going through those troubled years of trying to start a family taught me that life can throw you a curve ball at any time. You have the choice as to how you react to it. My choice was, and is, to try my hardest to make the best of it and look for the positive in any negative situation. I don't take my children for granted. I do my best to be an integral part of their lives. I participate as much as I can in their activities at school and activities outside of school, whether it is dance, baseball or hockey.

All my life I have been involved in athletics but I had never done anything that seemed to be out of the ordinary. Playing old-timers slow pitch and old-timers hockey, activities very common among many Canadian men in their 40's, was the extent of my physical activities. That changed in 2004 when I climbed to the summit of Mount Kilimanjaro. I had never climbed a mountain before and I had certainly never even thought about doing something like that. There was something that drove me to do it!

During our lives we typically settle into a comfort zone; a way of life that we are comfortable with. We do the same things with the same people and we take very few chances. It is very realistic to predict the results we are going to get in our lives because we keep doing the same things the same way. A friend of mine, John Kanary, once said "If you keep doing what you've always done, you will keep getting what you've always got."

Many of our dreams are just that — they are dreams because we only dream about them instead of

My First View of Mount Kilimanjaro, Tanzania, Africa.

turning them into goals and taking action towards attaining them. Whether it is staring your own business, making cold calls or standing in front of one hundred people to make a speech. You need to step out of your comfort zone in order to achieve what you dream of. Taking that first step can be very challenging because we know the edge of our own comfort zone and it is uncomfortable to be outside of that zone.

The climb of Kilimanjaro inspired me to continue to climb. It taught me to think big and have the confidence that I can achieve more in my life. My next climb after Kilimanjaro would be two years later to the Base Camp of Mount Everest. If you would have told me four years ago that I would have climbed both Kilimanjaro and to the Base Camp of Everest, I would have said you were nuts. There was nothing at all in my life, at that time, to suggest that I would be climbing mountains.

In the last number of months many people have suggested that I write this book. My immediate response was that I was not an author. I would tell people, "It's not going to happen. I'm not John Boy Walton. I'm not going to sit and write for an hour before I go to bed at night. It's not going to happen." (John Boy Walton was the main Character in the television series The Waltons from the early 1970's, who had aspirations of becoming a writer). Once I changed my thought process and realized that I could write a book, the dream of writing this book became a goal. I became emotionally involved in the goal and began to take action towards its completion; I began to start writing. As I sit here and write this preface, I can't help but think that just four weeks ago, the idea of writing a book was hard for me to imagine.

This book is called *Journey To The Top* because each of us are on our own journey to our own "top." One of my "tops" was to the top of Mount Kilimanjaro, and then it was to Everest Base Camp. Your top, or summit, may be to double your sales results, leave your corporate job with a pension, to start your own consulting business or to build your dream home. Whatever your "top" is, you will embark on a journey towards its accomplishment.

My journey to Base Camp taught me various lessons. My intent is to share with you this journey and to share the lessons I learned so that you can apply these lessons to the journey that you are on, today and in the future.

Two days from the summit of Mount Kilimanjaro.

"The difference between school and life?
In school, you're taught a lesson and then given a test.
In life, you're given a test that teaches you a lesson."

— Tom Bodett

Don't Be Afraid
To
Dream Big

February 15th, 2003 started out like an ordinary day for me. I got out of bed, shaved, showered, and got dressed and ready to go to work. I went downstairs and had breakfast with my wife Julie, our eight year old daughter Sydney and son Scott who was seven. Like any other typical day, I got into my car at 8:30 and drove to the office in downtown Hamilton. This day was starting off as a fairly basic day for John Stewart. Nothing was happening out of the ordinary that would have told me otherwise. It was about 10:30am, my day took a little bit of a change and marked a point in time where an email would inevitably change my life and the way I look at things in life. The email came from a colleague of mine, Laurie Mackie. I had known Laurie quite well for about ten years. She was a mother with two daughters. In her email she described a dream and a vision. I wasn't overly surprised to get such an email from Laurie because I knew of her strong faith and her willingness to give back to her community.

Her dream was to climb to the summit of Mount Kilimanjaro in Tanzania, Africa. At 19,340 feet above sea level, it is the largest free standing mountain in the world. Her vision was to raise money, over $250,000, for charity. I read the email once; I read it a second time, then my hand went to my mouse and I clicked on the reply button and I simply typed, "Laurie, we need to talk, I am seriously interested in doing this", then I clicked the "send" button. Within those five minutes, I had virtually committed myself to do something that I had never done before. I had never even thought of climbing a mountain my entire life, until that moment. I sat back in my chair and I thought, "Hmm, I have to go home and explain this to Julie."

That night at dinner, I was contemplating how I was going to tell my wife about today's events. Julie and I talked to the kids about their day as usual. We asked how their day went, what the best part of their day was and if anything interesting happened at school that day. When there was a break in the conversation I asked Julie, "Hey Hon, guess what I plan on doing next year?... I am planning to Climb Mount Kilimanjaro!" After explaining where Kilimanjaro was, Julie naturally asked me "why?" I explained, "Laurie is organizing a fundraiser in order to raise money for ALS (Lou Gehrig's Disease) research in honor of Jim Allen." Jim Allen was a colleague of ours who passed away from ALS the previous year, after being diagnosed with it just eight months earlier.

I knew at that moment she wasn't taking me seriously, she thought this was just another idea that would pass. After a few weeks of talking about it, training and talking to corporate sponsors, Julie finally realized that I was serious. I was going to do something that I had never done in my life. Many other people didn't take me seriously either. Why should they? I didn't work out, I didn't hike or like to go camping. Why would I suddenly have the desire to climb a mountain that is 19, 340 feet above sea level, where the oxygen at the summit is approximately half of what it is at sea level?

After a few weeks, others began to realize that I was serious; I started to get asked questions like, "Why climb a mountain?" "Why not sell raffle tickets, hold a dance or have a car wash?" There are many "normal" ways to raise money; but climb a mountain? I couldn't answer that question; I did not know the reason why. It took me nine months to realize that the reason was to become a better person, a better father and a better husband.

Our climb was led by Wally Berg. Wally, who owned and operated Berg Adventures International in Canmore Alberta, was one of the most respected guides in the mountaineering world. Wally has guided many people, all over the world ,to climb mountains. He has climbed to the summit Mount Everest four times and is world-renowned for his expertise, knowledge and mountaineering accomplishments. Wally's skills in planning, organizing, and guiding successful mountaineering expeditions have established him as one of world's leading expedition leaders. His passion for climbing and keen desire to give clients life changing experiences they would never forget, places Wally in a select group of people. He touches the lives of those that he guides, and his modest soft spoken manner leaves an indelible mark on those that get to know him.

During my climb of Kilimanjaro, Wally had told me that mountaineers have short term memories. What he meant was that during your toughest moments you tell yourself that you will never do anything like that again. While we were on our last leg approaching the summit, I was out of breath and totally exhausted, thinking to myself "Why in the world am I doing this? This is nuts. This is the most difficult thing I've done in my entire life. I will never do anything like this again in my life." That was when I reached my toughest moment. I kept going and pushed myself, and at 7:00am I was on the summit of Mount Kilimanjaro

It was March 8th 2004, and we were back down off the mountain. We had arrived back in our hotel in Arusha, and each of us had gone back to our rooms to clean up and shower. When you have been on Mount Kilimanjaro for eight days, this is really something you want to do! After everyone was cleaned up, we met in the lounge in the lobby of the hotel, to have a celebratory drink. There were thirteen of us. We were sitting and chatting, and Laurie had said, "I have an idea. Why don't we all go around one by one, and tell the rest of the group what we've learned from this journey."

So, one by one, we went around the room. It was very emotional, tears were obvious in the eyes of several of us. When it came time for me to speak, I said, "I can't tell you what I've learned to this point

Everest from Nameche Hill.

because I don't know. It's too soon, I can't articulate it, but I can say," as I looked at Wally, "you were right, mountaineers do have short term memories." A smile appeared on his face; he knew what I was going to say next. "I vow that I will climb another mountain to raise money for charity!"

With that thought in my mind, the idea of "Climb For Kids" was born. I would travel to Nepal, climb to the Base Camp of Mount Everest to raise money for Big Brothers Big Sisters. In the space of just over one year, from the time Laurie had sent me that fateful email, to the time I was sitting in the lounge in Arusha, I had made the decision and had climbed my first mountain. Now I found myself planning to do it again!

Instead of responding to Laurie's original email I could have ignored it and not acted on the idea of doing something different. The idea of dreaming big and doing something outside of my comfort zone had led me to a stage in my life full of excitement and accomplishment. It was truly life changing.

On April 29th, I began my journey to Everest Base Camp. Traveling with me was a neighbor, Doug Welland, as well as his twenty one year old son Tim. Doug was a retired economics professor and a self described Himalayan junkie. He is fascinated with the Himalayas and the Mount Everest region. Tim was an economics student at the University of Michigan.

While playing road hockey, in front of our house one afternoon with my son Scott, Doug stopped by on his way home from work. We spoke for a few minutes about my journey up Mount Kilimanjaro. When I explained to Doug that my next adventure was to Everest Base Camp, he enquired if he could join me.

Celebration at the summit of Mount Kilimanjaro.

After numerous emails, phone conversations, logistical planning and a doctor's clearance, both Doug and Tim were joining me on the trip of a lifetime. For the next eight months we shared our dreams and excitement, and we talked about our training and fund raising as we prepared for our trip.

We would be joined on our trek by seven others from across North America. Jackie Berger, Jim Barr and Jim Haskins were all from Alberta. Roger Brookins was from Arizona. Erin Skowran from Colorado and Andy Veres (nicknamed Opus) from Georgia, both were with the U.S. Air Force. Lastly there was Dr. Charles Martin (Doc) a pediatrician from North Carolina. This was to be our team.

The most difficult thing about climbing to Base Camp is the altitude and the lack of oxygen. When you get to the Base Camp, which is 17,598 feet, there is about half of the amount of oxygen to breathe as there is at sea level. Acclimatizing the body to this lower level of oxygen is a must for survival. If you were to take a helicopter to Base Camp, you would very quickly develop an extreme headache, dizziness and stomach sickness. Within a few hours you would be dead.

Your biggest enemy as you ascend up towards Mount Everest is Acute Mountain Sickness (AMS). AMS usually occurs after a rapid ascent to high altitudes and can usually be prevented by ascending slowly, allowing the body to acclimatize and adjust to the lower levels of oxygen. The symptoms of AMS can be compared to having a hangover. AMS can progress to high altitude pulmonary edema (HAPE) or high altitude cerebral edema (HACE). HAPE is swelling and an accumulation of fluid in the lungs. With severe cases of HAPE people will literally drown from the fluid built up in their lungs. HACE is an excess accumulation of water which puts pressure on the brain and can result in a loss of consciousness and a coma.

Training for the trek to base camp prepares you for the physical exertion that is involved in hiking for six to eight hours a day, ascending the mountainous terrain. However, training cannot prepare you for the effects that the higher altitudes can have on your body. Some of the most fit athletes in the world have been forced back because of AMS. Mother Nature and the mountain itself have a tremendous influence on who succeeds and who does not. As a result, the best method for success is to ascend slowly allowing your body sufficient time to acclimatize. The trek to Base Camp is an eleven day journey with an additional five days for the descent.

Everest Base Camp, which is located at the foot of Mount Everest, is the area where expedition climbers set up their base of operations for their attempt to summit the world's tallest mountain. Climbers will live at Base Camp anywhere from six to eight weeks. Climbing Everest is a well orchestrated exercise. Climbers need to ascend the mountain through a series of camps, continuously getting higher and higher. This slow process is followed in an attempt to convince the body that it can survive on less oxygen in one of the most extreme environments on the planet.

The trail to base camp travels through the Khumbu valley in the Khumbu region of Eastern Nepal. This valley follows the fast flowing Dudh Koshi river which is created by the water flowing from the glaciers high up in the mountains. The roar of the river quickly becomes part of the landscape as you hear it for much of the trek to Base Camp.

The Khumbu region is home to the Sherpa people, who became famous to the world when they served as porters for Sir Edmund Hillary and Tenzing Norgay when they became the first to summit

Our guides, left to right: Ang Temba, Jetya, Min, Wally Berg, Nuru, Pemba.

Everest in 1953. The Sherpa are an ethic group of people who came to the Khumbu region in the 1600s from the East. In Tibetan, "shar" means east and pa means people. Thus the word "sharpa" or Sherpa means people from the east.

Sherpas are highly regarded as experts in mountaineering, having incredible physical endurance and a resilience to high altitude. They are extremely important to expeditions and trekkers on their way to Everest, serving as guides and porters. It is commonly felt that Sherpas have a genetically greater lung capacity which allows them to perform much better at high altitudes. This belief however can unfortunately lead climbers to take for granted the heartiness of the Sherpa and not watch for signs of mountain sickness. Many of the people who become ill at high altitudes are Sherpas. Although they adapt very well to high altitudes, they are not immune to the effects that high altitude has on the body.

The Sherpas were going to act as our team's guides and porters and I learned their true character very soon after meeting them. They were extremely hospitable, grateful, caring, and genuinely very nice people. The teachings of Sherpa Buddhism describe a spiritual understanding between all beings. Sherpas believe that when they die they will be reincarnated into another life. The better they treat others in their current life, the better off that person will be in their next life. This explains why the level of hospitality comes so naturally to the Sherpa people.

While in this region, often you will see signs of this gentle caring nature. As a way of saying thank you or showing appreciation, Sherpas will place their hands together in a prayer like fashion, give a slight bow and say "namaste". This means thank you, it means "I appreciate what you are doing". It means "I like your company here, I am grateful to you". They do this as a sign of true affection for what you have and to say thank you; to say welcome to my home.

The Khumbu valley on the way to Mount Everest is full of beautiful rhododendrons.

"We grow great by dreams."

— Woodrow T. Wilson

LESSON 2

Money and Possessions Do Not Make You Happy

Spending time with the Sherpa in their homeland taught me something about North American arrogance. As Westerners, we feel our traditions are diluting their long time traditions. We feel that we are forcing our ways too much on the Sherpas and we are modernizing them. That cannot be further from the truth. What is really happening is our traditions and ways of doing things are actually strengthening the Sherpa culture. They do not want to be like us. They are happy we are there because it brings tourism dollars and they are gracious people, but they don't want our western ways. Who are we to say that our lifestyle is better than theirs? Sure, we may have many more luxuries in our lives, but that does not mean we are happier than those that live with less. Money and possessions may make us more comfortable, but it does not necessarily mean we are happier. It is, I believe, the western ego of us "rich" North Americans that makes us think that way, but it is not that way at all with the Sherpa culture. Hey, I'm all for making money and having nice possessions in life, and I am also strongly in favor of living a happy fulfilling life. What good is all the money in the world if you are not happy?

When I am at home, typically at night Julie will go to bed before I do. I will stay up for another hour or so and go to bed anytime after 11:00pm. I'll be downstairs watching the news or a good documentary. Often she will say to me "Oh Hon, by the way, before you come up, can you change the loads in the washer and dryer? Put the darks that are in the washer into the dryer, and then put the lights that are on the floor into the washer with a little bleach." Hey, I am a guy. What do you think is my first reaction? I'm thinking to myself; "Why are you giving me more jobs to do?" I'm not the type that will joyously jump to my feet and proclaim my love for my dear wife by saying; "Oh, Julie by all means I'll do it. I'll be glad to do it. What I am watching on TV isn't that important; I'll run downstairs to the basement right now and do it for you." I'm being facetious here; I will do it because it's important for me to help her out around the house.

A young Sherpa girl watches as we pass through her village.

But there are times when I get lazy and I would rather not do it. When Julie asks me about helping out with the laundry, I think of the Sherpa people that I saw doing their laundry. Sherpa women would carry a large wicker basket on their back with a large strap over their forehead holding the basket up. Inside, the basket is full of dirty clothes. The women walked to the Dudh Koshi River where they would squat at the river bank and repeatedly scrub their laundry. As they finished a piece they would drape it over a rock to dry. As you travel up the valley towards Base Camp, through the many villages that line the trail, you will quite often see clothes gently hung over the bushes in front of homes, drying in the daytime sun.

Money and possessions may make us more comfortable, but it does not necessarily mean we are happier.

A young Sherpa woman does her laundry at the banks of the Dudh Koshi river.

"We must accept life for what it actually is - a challenge to our quality without which we should never know of what stuff we are made, or grow to our full stature."

— Robert Louis Stevenson

LESSON 3

Obstacles are Part of the Game

The journey to Base Camp starts with a forty five minute flight from Katmandu to Lukla in an eighteen seat airplane. Lukla, which is 9,380 ft. above sea level, is a little town where most people begin and end their adventures in the Khumbu region.

After being the first person, along with Tenzing Norgay, to summit Everest in 1953, Sir Edmund Hillary realized that without the exceptional work of the Sherpa people, he would have never succeeded. Sherpas acted as guides and carried the tons of supplies to Base Camp that were needed for a successful summit. As a way of showing his never ending appreciation, Hillary made it his life work to give back to the Sherpa people by building schools and hospitals. An airport in Lukla would make it much easier to bring construction materials into the region and would eliminate the 6 day trek from Kathmandu to Lukla. In the early 1960's, Hillary built the airport so that materials could be flown into Lukla and then carried to the villages throughout the Khumbu region.

During the flight into Lukla you begin to see the big peaks of the Himalayas. Enthusiasm began to build in our plane as the peaks came into view. I looked over at Wally and without surprise saw him smiling and taking pictures of us as our excitement mounted. This was a flight that Wally had made dozens of times in the past. This was his favorite region in the world. He felt at home in the Khumbu region, often visiting old friends that he had climbed with in the past. This is where his true character really began to show itself; sharing in the joys and excitement of others as they began to embark on a journey they would cherish the rest of their lives.

About twenty minutes into the flight I began to feel nauseous. I reached into my waste pouch, sorted through all my medications and took out some anti-nausea tablets. Placing two in the palm of my hand I popped them into my mouth and took a drink from my water bottle. My thought was that this would surely fix my nausea, but little did I know…

The landing into Lukla was just ahead of us. The plane made a sudden sharp turn to the right. I could see the runway out the right side of the plane where I sat. I thought "Oh my God, it sure isn't very long." The runway was only fifteen hundred feet long. It rose on an angle sloping upwards as you landed. At the far end of the runway there was a large rock face of a mountain. As the wheels touched down, we all leaned towards the center aisle to look through the windshield to make sure we would stop in time. The plane immediately braked and we began to slow down, with the rock face coming closer and closer. We came to a stop and a collective sigh could be heard from the passengers on board!

The take-off at Lukla was just as thrilling as the landing. The plane races down the sloping runway gaining enough speed to become airborne, just as the runway comes to an end at the edge of a two thousand foot drop-off. The excitement continues as the plane then turns sharply to the left, avoiding the mountain range immediately on the other side of the valley.

We made it! We got off the plane and entered the small airport terminal. I wasn't feeling much better. I thought that getting out into the fresh air and moving around would have made me feel better. Well, it did not. I was still nauseous and now had shakes and chills. It was about seventy degrees outside and I found myself having to put on more clothing. We went into a lodge to have some tea while we waited for our porters to organize our bags for the trek. We stayed in the lodge for about ninety minutes. I had a little tea but had to lie down on a bench. Wally came to me and asked how I was feeling. "Not too good" I said.

The airport at Lukla. (photo by Doug Welland)

"John, you are definitely sick," he replied, "I'm in a short sleeve shirt, and I can't believe you're wearing all that." I had three jackets on, a wool hat and gloves — in seventy degree weather!

This trip had been over a year in the making. A year of preparation and training. The goal of reaching Base Camp became more than just a dream. I had made the decision and the commitment to accomplish it. Actions had been put in place to ensure the realization of that goal. On my desk in my office I had a large panoramic photo of Mount Everest, taken from the top of a mountain called Kala Patar. Everyday I would look at that picture and imagine myself sitting in that exact spot taking that very same photo. People would talk to me and ask me questions about how my plans were going. When I would climb stairs and climb a local ski hill as part of my training, I would imagine the exertion and exhaustion I would experience on the way to Base Camp. The goal of reaching Base Camp had captured me emotionally.

So there I was, half way around the world, in a little Nepalese village called Lukla, about to begin the trek that had consumed my thoughts for over a year, and I was sick. My only thoughts were "Great, this is just great. What can I do to feel better? All I can do now is just continue on and hope to feel better — soon."

As we began the trek along the trail towards Phakding, I had started to feel a little better. However, a short while later it hit me again. I knew at that moment that this was going to last longer than I had hoped. I was nauseous and weak. I had chills that would come and go; put a jacket on, take it off. I was carrying my 40 litre back pack on my back which weighed about twenty pounds. My camera bag with my still camera and video camera was strapped around my waist. As much as I wanted to put myself to the test and be self sufficient, I realized that it would be best if I put my ego aside for a while and let someone else carry my pack and camera bag.

Ang Temba Sherpa, our lead Sherpa guide, knew I was not feeling well. I thought he was the logical person to ask for help. "Ang Temba, would you mind carrying my pack and camera bag for me?" "Of course," he answered. The willingness to help and the compassion of the Sherpa became apparent to me immediately.

Ang Temba and his wife Yangzing lived in the village of Khunde and operated a lodge in Pangboche. On our way to Base Camp, as well as on our descent, they welcomed us all into their home. We were welcomed with sincere hospitality. The experience of sharing the customs of the Sherpa people with Yangzing and Ang Temba, made me realize that we shared a bond — a connection that will leave an indelible mark in my memories. Even though we lived on opposite sides of the world, the connection was genuine.

Ang Temba had traveled many times outside of Nepal, to the United States, Canada and Japan. This made him very comfortable in both worlds and allowed him to connect well with the people he climbed with. What made Ang Temba so memorable was his natural hospitality — with a western twist. He had the ability to communicate with climbers in a relaxed way as he taught them about the Sherpa. In 1991 he was a member of an all Sherpa team that reached the summit of Everest and since then he has acted as Sirdar, or chief Sherpa, for many expeditions on Everest.

Ang Temba Sherpa, our head Sherpa guide, always gave
me comfort to continue on when my strength was low.

We were about ninety minutes into our trek when the group had decided to stop for a brief rest and a drink of water. I was about five minutes behind the group, as my pace was slower. I eventually caught up with them beside a couple of small buildings. I sat down on the doorstep of one of the buildings. Various sets of eyes looked at me to see how I was feeling. I had my head down but I felt a gentle hand on my shoulder. It was Ang Temba. Very quietly and gently he asked, "How are you feeling John?" My first reaction was to break into tears. The thoughtfulness and compassion of this new friend had overcome me. There I sat feeling lousy and this man in his late thirties, who I had only met thirty six hours earlier, was having an effect on me that I had never experienced before. An effect that I would never forget for the rest of my life. I knew that I was in very capable hands.

"I can't let people see me crying," I thought to myself. My sunglasses were securely on my face so my next thought was as long as my tears don't fall down my face below my glasses nobody will notice. That didn't help. I could see the look on the faces of some of the others. Doug asked how I was doing. As he put a hand on my shoulder he reminded me that we were going to "high-five" at Base Camp. Eight months earlier when I had emailed Doug the details about the trek, trying to convince him to join us; I made a promise to him that we would "high-five" at Base Camp. Jim Haskins knew as well that I was feeling terrible and encouraged me to "hang in there Buddy."

As we continued on, my thoughts were beginning to challenge me. I had become scared and angry, thinking, "How many more days of this crap do I have to put up with?" I didn't want to be there. I did not think of turning around to go home; I just kept moving forward believing that at some point I would feel better. However, I missed my family terribly and I wanted to be at home. As I thought of Julie,

Sydney and Scott I would cry some more. I was walking alone, with Ang Temba about 20 feet behind me, mumbling to myself, "I love you guys so much; I wish you were here right now so I could give you each a hug."

The effect of higher altitudes was beginning to have an effect.

As we approached the lodge, where we were to stop for lunch, we had to climb about seventy five steps. Exhausted, I slowly climbed each step one by one. Focused on each step one by one, I slowly ascended to the top of the hill. I passed by the rest of the group at the entrance to the lodge and immediately found a bench that I would call home for the next ninety minutes. The others ate their lunch as I rested. Eating lunch was the last thing on my mind.

We arrived in Phakding late that afternoon, which would be our home for the night. Entering into Phakding requires a crossing of the Dudh Koshi River on one of the many suspension bridges that arch across the river. This would be my first attempt at one of these high swaying bridges, that mark the landscape throughout the journey to Base Camp. How was I going to handle this crossing when I was not feeling well at all? With a renewed sense of confidence I began to cross the three hundred foot long bridge, which hung two hundred feet above the roaring rapids below. As I progressed across, I could feel the swaying of the bridge at my feet. As I walked across the bridge would begin to sway like waves on water. To my surprise I made it across without incident, despite how I had been feeling. For the remainder of the trip, crossing these bridges would provide some fun and excitement for me.

At Phakding, we sat in the lodge and had some tea which I hoped would make me feel better. Later, I would go to my room and lie down, drifting into a deep sleep for two hours. In what had only seemed like minutes, my roommate Jim Barr shook my foot announcing that it was time for dinner. My immediate thought was to not want anything; I just wanted to stay in bed. However, eating something would probably have been a good idea. Slowly I got out of bed and gingerly walked across the grass to the main lodge for dinner. My appetite was still non existent, but I did attempt to eat a bowl of vegetable soup. Wally asked how I was feeling and commented that he could tell I wasn't feeling well — simply by how quiet I was. For those that know me well, being quiet is not something I am known for… After struggling through half a bowl of soup and trying to participate in the dinner conversation, it was time for me to get back to my room and rest. The feelings of anger and fear had overcome me once again. How long was this going to last? How would I feel tomorrow? Was this going to last for the entire sixteen days of our trip? My mind was swirling with all these thoughts. That night would be the test.

My sleep that night was the best sleep I had in long time. When I awoke, immediately I knew that I was much better. The feeling of that "hangover" had gone away. With renewed enthusiasm I quickly dressed with an energy and spirit that seemed so distant to me the day before. I walked into the main lodge with a skip in my step that put a big smile on Wally's face. "John sure feels better this morning", Wally said. I ate my breakfast with excitement. I was so happy to be feeling better knowing that the days to come would be much more enjoyable.

Having gotten through my bout of illness, I learned that Roger had a terrible night. He had been feeling quite sick. Eventually the decision was made that he would have to stay in Phakding until he felt

One of the many suspension bridges we needed to cross.

better. However, he would soon discover that he needed to head back down to Lukla so he could return directly home to Arizona. The mountain had spoken; this would not be Roger's time.

The remaining days of the trek were much better than the first day; however they didn't go with out their challenges. The effect of the altitude would still be present as we ascended higher and higher. I did not have my usual appetite for about three days. I had slight headaches, nausea, exhaustion, nervous anxiety and feelings of doubt that would come and go from day to day. The thought of "What am I doing here?" would enter my mind more than once. These feelings were not exclusive to me — others in the group were also experiencing similar feelings.

Having spent many days with Wally, our leader, he became a father figure — the one that you would go to and share these feelings. After hearing these concerns, his common response would be, "Don't worry about it, you're worrying too much. You'll be fine." My inner thoughts would say, "What do you mean don't worry about it? I'm half way around the world in the middle of the Himalayas on a trail and you're telling me 'don't worry about it?'" A natural reaction I supposed…

A few more days into our journey, I began to realize why Wally had responded to us in that way. One particular afternoon when Wally and I were alone sitting in a lodge drinking tea, I had again explained to Wally what I was feeling in my body as we were continuing to ascend into the thinner air. Anticipating his usual response of, don't worry about it, he instead told me something that taught me a great lesson, not only about mountain climbing but also in life, in general. He simply said to me, "Yea, I know what you mean." I thought about that for the next little while and finally realized what he had truly meant.

He had experienced the exact same feelings; the only difference was that he did not worry about it because he realized that it was part of the game. There will always be obstacles that you need to overcome. When you climb to altitude you are going to have these feeling regardless of how experienced you are. However, the more experience you have, the easier it is for you to deal with them.

You may find yourself in a period of your life, perhaps you have left your corporate job and you are now starting your own business. Or maybe you are simply planning on building a deck in your backyard. We all have goals that we want to accomplish which will require us to leave our comfort zone: increasing your sales, buying a new house, ending a relationship, being promoted at work or making the decision to finally retire. Do you have the courage to leave your comfort zone? What is really holding you back?

Think back to a time, a time when you did something that made you stretch yourself. Something that made you leave the comfort of doing what you had always done. Were there obstacles? Yes. Were you able to overcome them? Almost always, yes.

Wally had taught me that there would always be obstacles. They would present themselves and they needed to be overcome. It would have been easy to have turned around and gone home that first day when I had not been feeling well, I could have quit.

We always face challenges and obstacles. Understanding ahead of time that they are going to happen, and by keeping focused, staying calm and working through them, you will break through and achieve what it is you had set out do. There is a well known saying that I love;

There is no growth in your comfort zone, and no comfort in your growth zone.

If you stay in your comfort zone, you will never experience growth. And, if you leave your comfort zone to pursue what it is you truly desire, you will certainly experience discomfort. Keep the destination in mind!

As we continued to climb towards Base Camp, I discovered that there would be a series of "setbacks" that we would encounter. As we ascended higher up into the Khumbu Valley, these "setbacks" were in the form of losses in elevation. As you climbed higher up the valley, following the Dudh Koshi River, the trail would periodically cross the river to the other side of the valley. When climbing these mountains, ascending fifteen hundred feet up the side of the mountain means that you have gained fifteen hundred feet of the seventeen thousand-five hundred feet that it takes to reach Base Camp. Logically you know that the higher you go, the closer you are to the goal. Gaining altitude makes you feel that you are making progress. And then it happens… You realize that you have to cross the river. How do you cross the river? You cross the river on a suspension bridge. But the suspension bridge is not fifteen hundred feet above the river; it might be one or two hundred feet above the river. So if we are now at fifteen hundred feet, guess where the bridge was… We now had to descend down to where the bridge crossed the river. Going down to the bridge was not a big deal, but once you cross the bridge you soon realized that you had to go back up the other side of the valley. You begin to think "wait a minute; I just spent about three hours this morning gaining fifteen hundred feet — only to loose it crossing the river. I now have to go back up? What's going on here? Why can't this trail just stay on one side of the river?" These were natural thoughts of frustration, but once we understood that these losses of altitude were part of the game, we overcame those thoughts. As we continued the trek to Base Camp, these bridges soon became a source of comic relief. We began to laugh about it, which became our way of dealing with it. But that was simply frustration — another obstacle that we had to deal with. Our experience had taught us we had to cross the river, and every time you crossed a bridge, you lost altitude that has to be regained. That was that.

Ama Dablam

"Courage and perseverance have a magical talisman,
before which difficulties disappear and obstacles vanish into air."

— John Quincy Adams

LESSON 4

The Results in Your Life are a Reflection of Your Conditioning

We trekked slowly through the Khumbu Valley for eleven days, with two days of rest in order to acclimatize. After a few days of traveling through villages, I finally noticed that there were no roads. I had not seen a single wheel; I hadn't seen a cart, buggy, wheelbarrow, bicycle, or automobile. After sixteen days total trekking to Base Camp and back, no wheels were to be found. Something as simple as a wheel, which we take for granted everyday, was non existent.

If no wheels existed, then what was their main method of transportation? It was either back or yak. The Sherpa's method of transportation was by foot. Large loads were either carried on their back, typically in large baskets suspended by a strap on their forehead, or by yak — a large animal, with long hair hanging from their shoulders, native to the higher regions of Central Asia.

Witnessing, first hand, how these people walked everywhere, confirmed to me how much we depend on automobiles for travel. During summer weekends at the family cottage, I will often wake up early before the rest of the family and go down the road to get a newspaper at the corner store. When I get back to the cottage I pour myself a nice cup of coffee and read the morning paper. The store is about a mile away and takes roughly 20 minutes to walk there and back. Do I take our family dog, a Golden Retriever named Cooper, for a nice 20 minute walk in the morning to get the paper? No, I get in the family van and drive.

Just outside of the village of Namche, a young man approached me from the opposite direction along the trail. I estimated he was in his late twenties, five feet eight inches tall, a bit shorter than I was, and probably weighed about one hundred and sixty pounds, which was quite a bit lighter than me. Amazingly, tied together and strapped to his back, was a huge load of lumber to be used for construction in his village,

The yaks are packed with gear ready to continue our trek to Base Camp.

Nine 2x6's, twelve feet long.

which was further up the valley. There were nine pieces of two-by-six (inches) lumber, each one twelve feet long. He had tied them together in a bundle and then put them on his back with a strap that rested on his forehead. Wow, when I first saw this, I thought that if I was to be building a deck in my backyard, this would typically be the size of lumber I would use for the joists and frame. If the lumber store delivered it and dropped it in my driveway, I would carry them into the backyard, at most, two at a time. I certainly wouldn't be able to carry nine of them up a mountain.

Shortly afterwards, we took a rest in the same area this young man with the lumber was resting. As I rested, taking deep breaths of exhaustion, which were common to trekkers, I studied this young man as he sat quietly on a rock at the side of the trail. He was not breathing heavily at all. I soon realized that there was a major difference between us, aside from the obvious difference in physical conditioning. Not only had he physically conditioned himself to allow him to carry such a heavy load, he had mentally conditioned himself as well.

It appeared effortless for him. It was a way of life for him. My mental and physical conditioning, since birth, had instilled in me that there were certain ways to do things and certain ways not to do things. We transport lumber by truck, not by carrying it on our back. It would not be possible for me to condition myself to carry lumber this way because I did not need to. I had alternatives. Throughout our lives, we condition ourselves both physically and mentally based upon our experiences, environment and what we desire in our lives. If you want something badly enough, enough to be emotionally connected to it, you will condition yourself to receive it. Too often we condition ourselves such that our goals are only faint dreams; dreams we only fanaticize about. We have many dreams we never turn into goals. Those dreams

A group of porters carry heavy loads along the trail.

need our focus! When we focus our thoughts on a goal, we become emotionally involved and place steps of action that create progress towards the realization of our goal.

If you want to increase your sales results, don't just dream about increased sales, turn it into a goal. Focus your thoughts on actually increasing your sales. Become emotionally involved in increasing your sales and make plans to do it, then take action towards it. Make the decision that you CAN do it. Stop dreaming about it. Believe in yourself and take the required actions necessary to achieve it. You can condition yourself to achieve something if you want it badly enough. Attract it and act on it!

A view from Ang Temba's lodge in Pangboche.

"Plans are only good intentions unless they immediately degenerate into hard work."

— Peter F. Drucker

The Realization of
Your Goals
Appears Gradually

The first big peak that came into view was the mountain called Thamserku. We were on the trail with a ridge to our right and the river on the left. As the ridge started to become smaller, Thamserku began to emerge from behind the ridge. What a spectacular sight! You could feel the excitement in the group. Camera bags were quickly opened and all you heard was the sound of cameras taking pictures of the awesome view. What a beautiful mountain. Cameras were passed from person to person so that everyone could have a picture posing in front of Thamserku.

We continued our walk and I continued to take picture after picture. As the ridge on the right became lower and lower, Thamserku became bigger and bigger. More posing and of course, more pictures were taken. It was like a curtain opening on a stage of natural beauty. I ended up taking twelve pictures of Thamserku, each picture becoming better than the previous. Each picture showing more of Thamserku than the one before. This was our first glimpse at the high peaks of the Himalayas. These mountains would become even more spectacular in the coming days, as we approached our destination.

The process of putting into action the steps necessary to reach our goals, will reveal challenges and obstacles that must be overcome. At first we may begin to doubt whether it is all worthwhile and whether or not we should continue towards our goal. Knowing that obstacles are part of the game, and knowing with confidence that these obstacles can be overcome, we can push on and continue along the path towards our desired outcome. Then, suddenly, the goal you were striving for starts to come into view. It is at that moment your energy and enthusiasm will regain strength, knowing that the effort you have put in has started to show results. The obstacles you have encountered and the doubts that went through your

My first view of the big mountains; Thamserku.

mind start to become a thing of the past. Now is the time to kick it into high gear and keep working, keep focused and enjoy the journey as things continue to unfold; just as you had imagined in your mind when you first started your journey towards your goal.

Another spectacular mountain view.

"It is for us to pray not for tasks equal to our powers,
but for powers equal to our tasks,
to go forward with a great desire
forever beating at the door of our hearts
as we travel toward our distant goal."

— Helen Keller

LESSON 6

Look Back at Where You Have Come From

When you are climbing these mountains at this stage, it is a non-technical climb - it is trekking. You do not need ropes; there are no carabineers that you use to tie onto. The challenge of getting to Base Camp is the physical exertion of trekking all day long and the affects of the altitude. I had realized from climbing Mount Kilimanjaro, that there are two ways to accomplish the task. One approach is to simply go straight ahead, without looking back and just keep marching on. Keep looking up and keep moving on. Keep your eyes focused on where you are going and keep moving forward, don't look back. People using this approach have an unwavering focus on their goal.

This first approach may be difficult for some, as it was for me. We all have different personalities, different strengths and weaknesses — we are all different. Whether it was the summit of Kilimanjaro or the trek to the Everest Base Camp, for me the goal seemed a long way ahead. So far ahead, that at times I could not even see it. Sometimes it was days away. When this happens, you may begin to feel that you are not making progress and frustration starts to set in. It becomes tiring because you are thinking, "Man, I'm not making any progress here. This is brutal. I'm absolutely exhausted and I still have all this way to go. It is constantly up, up and up."

So how does this relate to everyday life? There is a second approach… I know people that are so focused on their goals, they never look back. They are so driven by the goals they are focused on. All they focus on is what they have yet to achieve. What I like to do, whether I'm climbing or working towards a goal in other areas of my life, is every now and then, just stop, turn around and look where I've come from. This gives me the confidence that I'm heading in the right direction.

When I am on a mountain, tired, and feeling like I have made no progress, I simply stop and look behind me. By looking back at where I've come from I can say to myself, "Wow, look at the ground I have gained since I crossed that river a couple of hours ago." I realize that I've come a long way, I am no longer frustrated and I can see the progress that I'm making on my journey. My strength and spirit becomes renewed and I can turn back around towards the direction of my goal, continuing forward and feeling much better!

It is very important to learn that every now and then, in any aspect of your life — whether it's your career, a project you have committed to doing or whether it is something you have volunteered to do in your community — stop what you are doing and look at the progress you've made. Throughout our lives we may reach moments when we begin feeling that no progress has been made. We become frustrated and may even feel like quitting.

Reflect on a regular basis about what you have to be thankful for. Take an inventory of what you have accomplished in your life and the difference you have made in the lives of others. Some people have no clue what they have in life to be thankful for. They are so focused on what they want next, that they have lost an appreciation for what they have already accomplished. They do not know what they've accomplished because they have not looked back. All they are doing is looking ahead at what is in front of them.

Don't get me wrong, it is very important to focus on your goals, otherwise you may never get there. Periodically we just need to just stop and become aware of the progress we are making. As difficult as it is at times, with all the obstacles that you face, you may begin to think that your goals are so big that you are not making progress towards them.

I was speaking at a conference in Las Vegas in 2004, talking about the concept of taking an inventory of the things you have done in your life. Two days after returning home, I received an e-mail from a gentleman who said, "John, thank you very much for talking about that. I was so focused on my business, I didn't have a clue. My wife and I sat down and we discussed for an hour all that we had to be grateful for, and all the things we have in our lives. It gave us new perspective for our lives. We're so glad you brought that up. You have made a difference in our lives."

It's good to know there is more than one way to reach your goals.

"If you're climbing the ladder of life,
you go rung by rung, one step at a time.
Don't look too far up, set your goals high
but take one step at a time.
Sometimes you don't think you're progressing
until you step back
and see how high you've really gone."

— Donny Osmond

Keeping your eyes focused only on your goal can be frustrating. At times you will feel you are making no progress…

...by looking back, you will realize how much progress you have made, and you will renew your spirit and energy.

Thoughts While Walking Alone...

In the moments that I would be alone walking on the trail towards Base Camp, I was captured by the beauty around me. Each day as we ascended higher the landscape would morph into a new and wondrous beauty. There would be new mountains to see and new villages to travel through. The view of a mountain would change as you travelled past it throughout the course of the day. As each hour would pass, so too would the perspective of the landscape around you. It seemed that the higher you went, the more majestic your view became. I would constantly say to myself "Wow, this beauty just never ends." Just when you think it surely could not get any better, it would. With every ridge passed, your view changed. And with every day that would pass my thoughts would become deeper and more meaningful.

I began to think of a quote that has a lot of meaning to me. This is from Endicott Peabody who was the Headmaster from The Groton School in Massachusetts in 1900.

"For life - which is in any way worthy, is like ascending a mountain.
When you have climbed to the first shoulder of the hill,
you find another rise above you,
and that achieved there is another, and another still,
and yet another peak, and the height to be achieved seems infinity:
but you find as you ascend that the air becomes purer
and more bracing, that the clouds gather more frequently below than above,
that the sun is warmer than before and that you not only get a clearer view of Heaven,
but that you gain a wider view of earth,
and that your horizon is perpetually growing larger."

Our lives are like climbing a mountain. There are peaks that we will reach throughout our lives, and in between the peaks are valleys that we must go through. For every peak that we reach, we must travel through another valley. It is those valleys we face that will ultimately determine our character and the person we are.

My thoughts would turn to my family, life and career. I would think often of Julie, Sydney and Scott, and a tear would develop in my eye. The thought of my son Steven came to my mind. If he were with us today, who would he look like? Sydney and Scott would have a big brother. Would he have played hockey and baseball like Scott does? He would also be there to stand up for his little sister and brother in school...

My thoughts would then turn to the question of the type of person I was. What kind of father am I? What kind of husband and what kind of person? I began to realize that I was taking the love our family has for each other for granted. I know Julie and the kids know that I love them; however there is always room for me to show them more.

When the kids want my attention, whether it is to talk or to play and have some fun, I need to show them a little more interest instead of sometimes being too consumed with what was on my mind at the time. I need to develop an attitude that shows I'm interested in them. Sometimes I just don't have the time to spend with them, but there are other times that I do have the time, but it just isn't a priority for me. I better start making more time, because how is it going to feel when they don't have the time for me? The time we have to share with our kids as they grow and develop is precious and we can't take it for granted. The moments that I had, like these on the mountain, are moments that I will remember and look back upon to keep me focused on being the best father and husband I can be.

Along the trail with Cholatse and Taboche Peak in the distance.

"Life is a mirror and will reflect back to the thinker what he thinks into it."

— Ernest Holmes

When You Feel Down, Don't Quit Working Towards Your Goal

An interesting fact about Mount Everest, that most people do not realize, is that you cannot see the summit of Everest when you are at Base Camp. This is due to the camp being situated at the base of the western shoulder of the mountain. With this large mountain face right in front of the Camp, the angle hides the view of the summit. Because of this, a secondary goal for our team was to climb to the top of the neighboring mountain Kala Patar. Most trekkers who are making their way to Base Camp make this climb as it provides a tremendous view of Everest.

At just over eighteen thousand feet, Kala Patar is higher in elevation than Base Camp. It sits beside the small village of Gorak Shep, the last village before reaching Base Camp. It is a steady thirteen hundred and forty five foot uphill climb from Gorak Shep to the summit of Kala Patar. The motivation and prize for the climb up Kala Patar is the absolutely stunning unobstructed view of Everest. This was the photo opportunity of the trip! For days preceding our arrival at Gorak Shep, we would regularly talk of summiting Kala Patar and taking the "money shot." Talk about "living your dream, obtaining the goal…" There I would be, sitting in front of Everest, enjoying the moment. I would be sitting in the exact spot where the panoramic picture that was in my office had been taken. That picture had provided inspiration to me for over a year! I was going to live my dream!

We had trekked from Lobuche, in cloud cover, and arrived in Gorak Shep by noon. The plan was to climb to Kala Patar that afternoon. As we sat and drank tea outside, talking of our pending climb of Kala Patar, I felt drained of energy and had no enthusiasm to go anywhere. The sun was nowhere to be found. A bit demoralized, my thoughts were on how the "money shot" of Everest was not going to happen, due to the weather. Everest could only be seen from Kala Patar if the sky was clear.

As the sun sets on Ama Dablam, the moon rises overhead.

Sitting there, I felt sorry for myself. I looked over at Wally and said, "You know what? If it's not really clear, I'm not going to climb." He replied in a stern tone, "What?" I replied, "I don't feel like climbing if it's not going to be clear, we won't be able to take any good pictures so what's the point?" Immediately it was as if he had taken a baseball bat and whacked me over the head. He said to me, "John, you're not going to quit! I thought you stood up in front of people and told them that they could achieve what ever they wanted in their lives; to have the strength and courage to keep going. Now you're saying you're not going to go because you can't take a good picture?" Wally was absolutely right! I had talked about quitting because I did not feel that well. We had been going for 10 days and I was tired. He said, "John, you're not going to quit. You're going to go up that mountain, even if it is cloudy and you can't see a thing, you're going up there!" I looked at Wally with a humbled look and said, "Yeah, you're right, I'm going." Immediately, my attitude had changed and I was motivated to go as I found my renewed energy.

Immediately after lunch we began our climb of Kala Patar. The start of the climb was not too bad. We stopped part way up, to take pictures, when the summit of Everest first came into view. Both Erin and Doug were feeling quite tired and had decided to turn back. They wanted to save their energy for the last leg to Base Camp the next morning. The remainder of the team resumed climbing through thick clouds that had come over us. It had begun to cool and started to snow — I needed to retrieve my heavy down coat, wool hat and warm gloves from my back pack.

Up to this point my breathing had acclimatized quite well to the thin air. However, on this climb I began to feel the lack of oxygen as we steadily ascended higher and higher. When the body craves oxygen, the natural reaction is to breathe heavily in an attempt to acquire as much oxygen as possible.

As I began to see what I thought was the summit, my energy felt renewed, but this was brief. It was a false summit — a ridge viewed from below can look like the top but actually is not. When we reached the top of that ridge, it became apparent that we had much further to go. The huffing and puffing continued and we moved forward…

The actual summit soon came into view. But it was one of those things; it felt as though we just weren't getting any closer. Those feelings of frustration and exhaustion had set back in, it felt as though we were not making any progress. My breathing had become labored — I inhaled through my nose and exhaled through my mouth in a very deliberate breathing pattern. I developed a routine of counting two hundred steps out loud, and then leaning on my trekking poles to rest and take thirty deep breathes. I would then turn around to see the progress we had made. Then, two hundred more steps, thirty more deep breaths and turn around to see our progress. This became three hours of difficult trekking, step after step, huffing and puffing all the way. That went on and on and on and I would keep looking back. "Yeah, I'm making it, I'm making it, keep going, keep going." I never thought to quit! I always kept thinking "this is stupid, who signed me up for this?" My thoughts were the same as they were as I approached the summit of Kilimanjaro two years earlier. But I kept going, knowing that I was getting closer and I would make it. I had learned that this was just part of the process.

Up ahead was Opus, Doc along with the Sherpa guide Nuru. I had looked at Doc's pace to see if I had been catching up to him. Slowly the gap had been narrowing. I never looked at these climbs as any kind of race. There was no prize for the person that gets to top first. There had been many people there before me and there will be many people that get there after me. However, seeing that the gap was closing was further evidence that I was making progress — this gave me energy. Suddenly the summit came into

Nuru, Doc and Opus on the summit of Kala Patar.

view. I could see Opus, he had made it and was sitting on the summit; I still had a ways to go. With the summit in sight, I could feel my energy pick up. I kept my pace and continued on, one step at a time, still breathing heavy in a rhythmic pattern. I realized that I had not been counting the two hundred steps. I was feeling better; tired, but better. The summit was only fifty feet away. Opus and Doc were sitting waiting for me. The adrenaline kicked in and I quickly climbed the last few rocks with what seemed like no effort at all. Finally — I made it!

The summit was not very big. It was a flat rock about ten feet wide by twenty five feet long and sat on an angle, right on the top of Kala Patar. Doc and Opus were up there and I was the third one to arrive. I climbed onto the summit rock and crawled over beside Doc. I turned back around and immediately fell back with my head on Doc's shoulder and began to cry. "You did it man, you did it man," Doc said in a very comforting manner. The three of us just sat there, catching our breath, taking in the view. The conversation then turned to the wondrous environment around us.

The rock at the summit was tilted on about a thirty five degree angle. As I leaned over to my right to take off my back pack to get some water, I suddenly realized that I was right on the edge of the summit, looking straight down approximately seven hundred and fifty feet. "If I fall, I'm dead!", I calmly thought. There was as sense of peace and it really did not bother me. As I struggled with my back pack trying to get it off, Nuru had a hold of my leg, while Doc held me by the back of the pants. Doc said to me, "John, be careful." "I'm okay", I replied, "I need some water." I finally got it off and had a drink of water. I sat back up straight and thought to myself about why I was so at ease as I had leaned precariously close to the edge. There was just this unexplainable sense of calm while sitting at the summit with Doc, Opus and Nuru. I trusted them and I had no fears.

We could see the rest of the team getting closer. We had spent three hours climbing Kala Patar and it was normal for a climbing team to get stretched out. Within fifteen minutes or so, we were all at the top. I moved off the summit to make room so the others could sit on the summit rock. I looked down and saw three people coming up towards us at a very quick pace. It appeared that they were almost running. I asked Nuru who they were, as I pointed below us. "Oh, that's Pemba with our tea," he answered. I thought; I can't believe these people.

Sherpas drink a lot of tea and three of the Sherpa staff, Pemba, Mingma and Jetya were coming up the mountain to serve us hot tea. We were still breathing heavily, when Pemba came and asked, "Want some tea?" He wasn't even breathing hard, after having ran up the mountain. Pemba was holding the tea, Mingma had the mugs and Jetya was holding the cookies. So there we were, sitting drinking hot tea and eating cookies on the top of Kala Patar…

There was still a full cloud cover and I had sat there feeling sorry because it did not appear we were going to get any of those "money shots" of Everest. Everyone had arrived and was drinking their tea. What happened next was unbelievable… I honestly believe that Mount Everest said, "Okay folks, you've been good — you've struggled, you're here. It's now time that I show you what I really look like." And within a few short minutes, the clouds opened and we had clear skies. There she was! Mount Everest was sitting right in front of us in the clear afternoon light. Every camera came out!

Pemba serving tea on the top of Kala Patar.

We got back down off Kala Pattar just before dinner. I was the first down and joined Erin and Doug at the lodge. I wanted to share with them the experience at the summit of Kala Pattar. As I began to explain the adventure, I started to cry again. Doug put his arm around me and comforted me. I told each of them that I thought they had made the right decision to turn around and not attempt Kala Patar. We were there to visit Base Camp and they needed to preserve their energy for the next morning when we would finally arrive at Base Camp. When Wally arrived, I put my arm on his shoulder and gave him a slap on the back. I thanked him for encouraging me earlier in the day. I was tired, but I was sure glad that I made it up there.

The "money shot" of Everest!

The view of the mountains from the Thame Monestary.

"Success seems to be connected with action.
Successful people keep moving. They make mistakes, but they don't quit."

— Conrad Hilton

It's Not About
the Destination,
It's About the Journey

The approach to Base Camp.

The next morning we left for our final trek to Base Camp. We would spend a couple of hours there and then turn around to head back. Base Camp is situated at the foot of the Khumbu Icefall on a glacial moraine. It is comprised of large rocks and boulders that constantly shift as the Khumbu Glacier steadily moves beneath it. Expedition teams send Sherpas to Base Camp two days in advance to build tent beds. Due to the constant shifting of the rocks, new tent beds are built each climbing season. The large rocks and boulders are moved and chiselled in order to make a flat spot to erect a tent.

For four hours we slowly made our way to Base Camp travelling on top of the glacial moraine. We walked carefully on large rocks, each step deliberate and methodical in order to keep our balance and ensure secure footing.

As we approached Base Camp, I was surprised to see the number of tents erected in this temporary city. There were fifteen expedition teams there, all attempting to summit Mount Everest. Close to one hundred and fifty tents were scattered throughout the landscape. There were narrow sleeping tents, large square dining tents and large round communication tents; all in different colours with sponsor names printed on many of them.

There was a sense of excitement as we entered Base Camp late that morning. Some of the team proceeded further along as Tim and I waited for Doug, who was about 5 minutes behind. I could see that Doug was tired, an exhausted look covered his face. As he approached, he saw us waiting and his look turned to a look of joy, knowing that he had made it. Doug and Tim, father and son, embraced. I walked over to Doug, each of us feeling the emotion of the moment, and gave him a hug. "We did it, we did it!" Then, as planned eight months earlier, we proceeded to give each other a "high five".

The city of tents at Base Camp.

We continued on further into Base Camp amidst all the tents. The feeling was unlike our experiences to date. Expecting more thrill and excitement to our adventure, we soon discovered a contrasting experience. It was bleak. There was no feeling of energy or excitement here. Base Camp was the most inhospitable and unwelcoming environment I had ever been in. The people we met were quite pleasant, but I had this strange feeling that I did not want to be there. We had spent all this time to get here, and when we did, I somehow knew I didn't want to be there for long. We met some friends of Wally's who were there for a summit attempt. They were quite welcoming and were very friendly. I remember saying to Jim Haskins, "I couldn't imagine spending one night here, let alone six weeks!" It did not take him long to agree.

We each received a bagged lunch that had been prepared for us. The dining tent, that belonged to the group we were visiting, was full. Doug and I sat beside each other on a rock about ten feet away from the tent. We quietly ate our lunch without speaking a word to each other. Without much of an appetite, I ate what I could and sat with my head down, starting to think of my family. With a tear in my eye, I slowly removed a small plastic bag from my pocket and took out of it two fingernail clippings that were given to me, one from each of my children Sydney and Scott. They had asked me if I could bury them at Everest for them. I dug a small hole with my foot and delicately buried them so that a small piece of my children would always be at Mount Everest. Next, I gently picked up two small stones to bring home and put them in my pocket so that a piece of Mount Everest would always be with them. Wiping the tears from my eyes, I looked up at Doug and realized that I wanted to leave and get back to our lodge at Gorak Shep.

I asked Doug if he wanted to join me in heading back to Gorak Shep. He agreed without hesitation. I asked Wally if we could get a Sherpa guide to lead us back and as Nuru started to lead us back, I was surprised to see that five others were also ready to head back. We had only spent an hour there, but that was enough, we knew it was time for us to turn around.

Although the visit to Base Camp had been our goal for over a year, the visit itself was very anti-climactic. Some goals that we do reach in our lifetime are just that, anti-climactic. The excitement doesn't come exclusively from the realization of a given goal. The true excitement and feeling of accomplishment comes from the journey itself. It comes from the obstacles that present themselves along the way and the perseverance required to achieve your goal. There is a well known quote from an unknown source that says:

Success is a constant journey, not a destination.

Doug and I "high five" at Base Camp. (photo by Tim Welland)

The jagged peaks of the Himalayan Mountains.

"To finish the moment, to find the journey's end in every step of the road,
to live the greatest number of good hours, is wisdom"

— Ralph Waldo Emerson

Take Time
to Celebrate
Your Victories

The day after our arrival at Base Camp, we woke up early to a nice breakfast and then began our five day descent back down the valley to Lukla. We would later take the flight from Lukla to Kathmandu, before departing Nepal on our flights back to North America.

I had noticed on the journey down, that I had a totally different perspective on things, for two reasons. The first was that I felt much better and I was now handling the altitude. We were moving into lower elevations where the air was richer with more oxygen to breath. It was great to be breathing normal and I felt as though I was having the time of my life. The struggles were now behind me. We had reached Base Camp and I was on my way home. My appetite was back to normal after eleven days. Now, feeling much better, I was able to enjoy the surroundings so much more. I would find myself laughing along the trail and talking more to the people around me. My energy was back to normal and obstacles were nowhere to be found.

The second reason for my new perspective was that we were now travelling in the opposite direction — a familiar path, without unexpected events or anticipation of the unknown. The view of the mountains was different than during our ascent — a new perspective. Where I saw sunrises before, I now saw beautiful sunsets. This new perspective added excitement to our journey down. New experiences occurred each day, which simply added memories to such a wonderful journey.

For some of us, the realization of a goal that we have committed to means the end of one journey and the beginning of another. The success of my goal, reaching Base Camp, was not the end of the journey. The next five days, as we descended, were spent in celebration of what we had accomplished. I would

Celebrating a successful journey in front of the Tengboche Monestary.

look back at the obstacles faced. Having been sick, feeling scared, not wanting to be there, exhausted, losing my appetite and feeling defeated by the thought of not being able to get the "money shot" photo. Being able to reflect on those obstacles and how they were overcome, encouraged me to think about new goals that I wanted to achieve.

Perhaps, for some of us, when we reach a goal in our lives, we quickly move onto the next one without reflection on what it took to achieve that previous goal. So much can be learned by reflecting back. Looking at the obstacles faced. How did you feel? Did you want to quit? What kept you going? What did you learn?

I encourage you to celebrate the accomplishment of your goals. Enjoy it! Look at what you have accomplished. Celebrate it! Feel good about it! Don't let it go! That's what I did — I spent five days celebrating what I had done. It was absolutely awesome and it made the entire journey so much more complete. This was perhaps my most rewarding lesson!

During the time of celebration and reflection, start to plan your next goal. I began to think about "Climb For Kids" and the plan of making it an annual event. I envisioned that each year, a group of climbers and I would travel to Mount Kilimanjaro, raising money for Big Brothers Big Sisters. Thinking about what I wanted to do next, while still celebrating my most recent victory, gave me the motivation necessary to spring me into action towards my next goal. The obstacles faced on this journey, and how I overcame them, prepared me for accomplishing future goals in my life.

Feeling proud at Base Camp.

While thinking about this on the trail, I began to chuckle to myself and smile as I realized the effect that all this was having on me. Just a few days earlier, I was struggling up Kala Patar, thinking to myself, "Who signed me up for this? This is nuts. This is the most exhausting thing I have done in my life." Wally's words from Kilimanjaro three years earlier came racing back to me, "Mountaineers have short term memories."

As we approached Lukla, the realization that this journey was quickly coming to an end set in. There was a long set of steps to climb, just before walking through the concrete arch at the entrance to Lukla. I counted to myself the last sixty steps as the arch came into view. Walking through the village, my first thought was that there would be no more hills to climb, for that I was thankful.

We would leave Lukla first thing the next morning on our flight back to Kathmandu. I spent that afternoon relaxing in our lodge, reflecting on our journey. The experiences we had with the Sherpa; their hospitality, graciousness, loyalty and modesty. I thought back to my different mood swings. The times I was challenged mentally because I didn't want to be there. The fear and anxiety I experienced. Being sick on the first day, and again how I was able to overcome the various obstacles that I faced. I remembered the good times we had. The joy and triumph of doing something that I once thought was unachievable.

As one journey ends, another journey will begin. The first journey would be my trip back home to be with Julie, Sydney and Scott. I had missed them tremendously and I was very excited knowing that in a few days I would be home with them. There will be many other journeys in my life — some that I know of now, and others that will present themselves in the future. I look forward to what life has to offer in the future, knowing that my experiences of the past will help me enjoy each future journey.

Taking time to reflect as we descend down towards Lukla.

Since my return home, many people have asked me what I have learned from such an experience. Within each of us there lies a spirit; a spirit that has the ability to help us achieve whatever it is we dream of. A spirit that will allow us to live the life we desire. This spirit lies within each of us and is waiting to be released. The only thing holding back our ability to release this spirit is our attitude, lack of self confidence, negative thinking, and our inability to truly believe that we can live the life we dream of. There comes a time in our lives when we are able to set that spirit free; and that time is right now. What are you waiting for? Find the courage to set that spirit free and begin working towards whatever it is you want in life.

Celebrating on top of Kala Patar. (photo by Wally Berg)

"Courage is the first of human qualities because it is the quality which guarantees the others."

— Winston Churchill

4 Principles From the Lessons Learned

4 STEPS TO YOUR SUMMIT

Each of us is on a journey throughout our lives. These journeys take on many shapes and forms. They are the journeys towards our hopes and dreams for the future. What do you want to accomplish in your life? Where is your journey taking you? Are you making definite progress towards your goal? Or, are you stuck in your present circumstances, discouraged that you can not seem to get ahead in life? Is your journey even happening?

My journey to Everest Base Camp taught me many lessons. Upon reflection, those lessons caused me to develop the "Four Steps to the Summit." I define the summit as being the goal that you have chosen to pursue. The summit does not necessarily mean the summit of a mountain. However, the same principles apply whether you're climbing a mountain or striving to increase the results in your life. I hope these four steps help you to reach for your "summit"!

STEP ONE - Determine Your Summit

- Visualize what you want to achieve.

All of us have dreams — dreams of how we want to live, of what we want to achieve, how we want to feel and so much more. They remain only as dreams until they are turned into goals, followed by the decision to do something to make those dreams a reality. Within us all is the ability to achieve what we desire.

Ask your self these questions about your personal goals. What trip would I like to go on? What kind of car do I want to drive? Where do I want to live? What is important to me personally? What are my business goals? How much income do I want to make? What do I really want to do in my career or business? Determine in your mind exactly what is your desire. It's called dream building.

The first step in achieving what you want is to clearly visualize it. You must paint a clear picture in your mind. If you can not picture it in your mind you will never achieve it. Have you ever taken a drive in your car without know exactly where you are going? If you do not clearly know where you are going, then you will be aimlessly driving about. Put a picture on your bathroom mirror of what you want. Write down on a card the income you want to earn and keep that card in your pocket. Have a clear picture in your mind of your goals and keep them right in front of you.

STEP TWO - Decide you can do it.

- Develop a "can do" attitude with an unwavering belief.

There is only one thing that can restrict our ability to achieve our goals — belief. Our beliefs determine how we live our lives. We have social beliefs, personal beliefs and business beliefs. All of these beliefs have been developed throughout our lives based upon our environment, how we have been raised, the people we associate with and our many experiences.

If you do not truly believe you can achieve your goals, you are right. If you do not believe in yourself, you will actually sabotage your success without even knowing it. The subconscious is a powerful tool, be careful how you program it. What goes in, is generally what comes out. Constantly reinforce your belief — associate with positive uplifting people and feed your mind with information that is in sync with your beliefs.

You must have a steadfast belief that you can achieve what it is that you want. On a constant basis, believe that you can do it. Eventually that belief will become habitual, and there will be nothing that will convince you that you can not do it. This is how you protect your dreams. Your thoughts must be positive. When a negative thought enters your mind, be aware of it and immediately replace that thought with a positive one. Keep that "can do" attitude alive!

STEP THREE - Develop a plan

- Know how to get there. Don't just dream, take action.

You now have a clear vision of what you want and you believe you can achieve it. Now you need a plan of action towards attaining your goal.

Write down the answers to these questions:

What has to happen for me to achieve my goal?
What do I have to do differently than I am doing now?
What do I need to plan in order achieve what I want?
What tools do I need?
What support do I need and who do I need help from?

Thinking about these questions and being truthful to yourself will identify what you need to do in order to move closer to your goal.

Knowing what to do means nothing, unless you do what you know. You need to act! Start by making a list of the actions you need to take.

What do I need to commit to in the next week?
What do I need to commit to in the next month?
What do I need to commit to in the next year?

It is not necessary to start with an overwhelming amount of things to do. Start small. What can you do immediately that will move you closer? As an example, if your goal is to increase your sales results, why not make three extra sales calls today? If you want a new car, go to the dealership on your way home, look at the cars and get a brochure.

The most important thing you can do is start doing something today that will move you closer. It is very easy to get in the habit of putting things off and then realize that another year has gone by and you are no closer to reaching your goal than you were last year.

STEP FOUR - Persist in your journey

- Obstacles will get in your way. Keep focused on your goal.

What would you do if you hit an obstacle on the very first action you took towards your goal? Would you quit? I sure hope not. Obstacles are inevitable. Stuff happens. No one ever said that life would be easy.

Persistence is more important to the success of your goal than most talents. Many people, who were not the most talented, persisted in their goal to become extraordinary. Did you know that Michael Jordan was cut from his high school basketball team? A newspaper fired Walt Disney for not having good ideas.

Achieving goals in life requires commitment, not just an interest. Being committed will keep you focused and allow you to work through the obstacles you will face. If you are only interested, the first major road block that gets in your way will cause you to turn and retreat.

The challenges that appear need to be kept in perspective. Do not let something minor become so major that it will sabotage your efforts and convince you to give up. Treat them as a temporary set back that, at most, will only slow you down. Colonel Harland Sanders, who started Kentucky Fried Chicken, was rejected over 1000 times before his recipe for fried chicken was finally accepted.

It is also important to understand that set backs are not personal. They are not a reflection of a character flaw you have; but instead are simply challenges that show you the need to modify your approach. You can learn from these set backs, inevitably they are providing lessons, that if learned, will help you to move closer towards your goal.

Determine, decide, develop and persist!

"One last time together" – Photo by Wally Berg.

"Persist and persevere, and you will find most things that are attainable, and possible."

— Lord Chesterfield